Contents

Imperial War Museum London
Lambeth Road
London SE1 6HZ
Tel 020 7416 5000

The Churchill Museum
and Cabinet War Rooms
Clive Steps, King Charles Street,
London SW1A 2AQ
Tel 020 7930 6961

Imperial War Museum Duxford
Duxford Airfield,
Cambridge CB2 4QR
Tel 01223 835000

Imperial War Museum North
Trafford Wharf Road,
Trafford Park
Manchester
M17 1TZ
Tel 0161 836 4000

FOREWORD

The Imperial War Museum is very proud of the fact that it is responsible for HMS *Belfast*. She is a fine ship and a unique and powerful reminder of Britain's naval heritage. As such, she plays an important part in the Museum's work of recording and explaining the history of war in the twentieth century and in highlighting the experiences of millions of ordinary people - soldiers, sailors, airmen and civilians - who were caught up in the great conflicts of their time. For in the final analysis, the story of HMS *Belfast* is primarily one of human endurance and endeavour.

The same is true at our other sites: the underground Cabinet War Rooms, from which Winston Churchill and his advisers directed the nation's efforts during the Second World War; Duxford, the famous Battle of Britain airfield; and the Museum's Main Building in Southwark, which houses the world's greatest collection of artefacts, documents, film, photographs, and works of art devoted to the subject of war in the twentieth century.

Preserving a ship of this size and complexity is a costly and time-consuming business. HMS *Belfast* successfully completed a dry docking, coinciding with the Millenium, which required her to be towed through the English Channel to Portsmouth and back in the space of a month. I hope that you will enjoy your time on board and that you will want to visit the Museum's other sites as well.

Robert Crawford

Robert Crawford
Director - General
Imperial War Museum

INTRODUCTION

HMS *Belfast* is a cruiser. She was launched in 1938 and served with distinction in both the Second World War and the Korean War. She is now the only surviving example of the great fleets of big gun armoured warships built for the Royal Navy in the first half of the twentieth century and the first ship to be preserved for the nation since Nelson's flagship, HMS *Victory*.

When delivered in August 1939, *Belfast* represented the high-water mark of British cruiser development and her retirement from active service in 1965 brought down the final curtain on a long line of vessels built to protect the Empire's trade routes during the period of Britain's maritime ascendency.

As you tour this great warship you will probably be amazed by her sheer size and the complexity of the machinery and equipment which made HMS *Belfast* one of the most powerful vessels of her type afloat. But please spare a thought for her crew. At the height of her operational service at the end of the Second World War, HMS *Belfast* was home to over 950 officers and men. Apart from the threat posed by enemy action, whether from German surface warships, U-boats, aircraft, mines or torpedoes, HMS *Belfast*'s crew also had to confront the ever-present menace of that most remorseless and pitiless of all enemies - the sea. Packed into her unyielding, yet all too vulnerable steel hull, her crew endured the most uncomfortable and, at times, squalid conditions as HMS *Belfast* cruised the oceans of the world in the twilight of Britain's Imperial epoch.

In all her many and varied aspects, HMS *Belfast* is a vital and enduring reminder of the reality of naval warfare in the twentieth century. As Director, it is my pleasure to welcome you on board in the certain knowledge that your support will help to ensure that future generations will be able to experience the wonder of this great, historic warship.

Brad King.

Above Robert Crawford, Director General of the Imperial War Museum

Above Brad King, Director of HMS *Belfast*

Left, outside front cover, inside front cover and outside back cover
Photographs: Glyn Williams

Page 1 black & white shot
IWM Neg. No. A 6872

YOUR VISIT TO HMS BELFAST

Welcome on board HMS *Belfast*!

The purpose of this chapter is to help you to find your way around this huge and complex warship and to get the most out of your tour. Even though at least half of the vessel cannot be opened to the public for reasons of safety, there are still nine decks to explore and it is all too easy for visitors to get confused and to

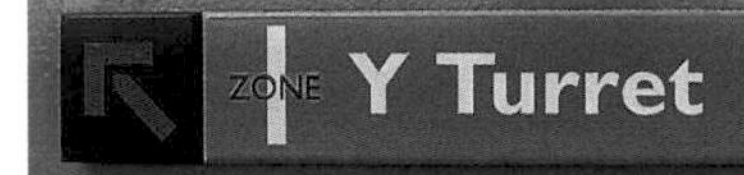

miss out on seeing key areas of the ship.

To help you find your way around HMS *Belfast*, the ship has been divided into eight zones. These are detailed opposite and in the ticket/guide leaflet which is made available to all visitors. Though you are free to plan your own route through the ship, it is suggested that you visit each zone in sequence, starting from the ship's Quarterdeck (Zone 1).

Each zone is colour coded and you will encounter directional signs at frequent intervals during your tour. In addition, you will find a number of Video Information Monitors, explaining certain technical aspects of HMS *Belfast*'s operation, which also include information about the visitors' route. If you should get lost, please ask a member of staff for directions.

The Ship's Main Engine Throttle.

Your tour will take you from HMS *Belfast*'s Quarterdeck up to the top of her Bridge and all the way down to her massive Boiler and Engine Rooms, located well below the ship's waterline. On your way, you will be able to see inside her triple 6-inch Gun Turrets; operate her light anti-aircraft guns; explore the heavily armoured Shell Rooms and Magazines, and experience what life was like for her crew by visiting the cramped Messdecks, Officers' Cabins, Galley and Sick Bay.

Toilets

Toilets are situated close to the Quarterdeck (where visitors come on board) in Zone 1, and towards the bow of the ship in Zone 3.

Meeting Point

The Quarterdeck is the suggested meeting point for all visitors, either boarding or leaving the ship. A member of staff is on duty here at all times and a broadcast system is available, if necessary, to pipe an emergency message to visitors.

Access for the Disabled

The Imperial War Museum is a member of the Museums and Galleries Disability Association. Every effort is made to make HMS *Belfast* as accessible to disabled visitors as possible. A wheelchair lift provides access to the ship, with entry to the upper deck via special ramps. A disabled toilet has been installed close to the main entrance.

Virtual Tour

Our Virtual Tour can be accessed on board at a special terminal on 2 Deck or by following the links on our web-site **www.iwm.org.uk**. In it you can explore many of the main areas of the ship including the Boiler, Engine and Shell Rooms plus some areas not usually accessible to the public.

Please be careful and do mind your head when using the ship's ladders. Children must be supervised at all times when exploring the ship. We hope that you will enjoy your visit to HMS *Belfast*.

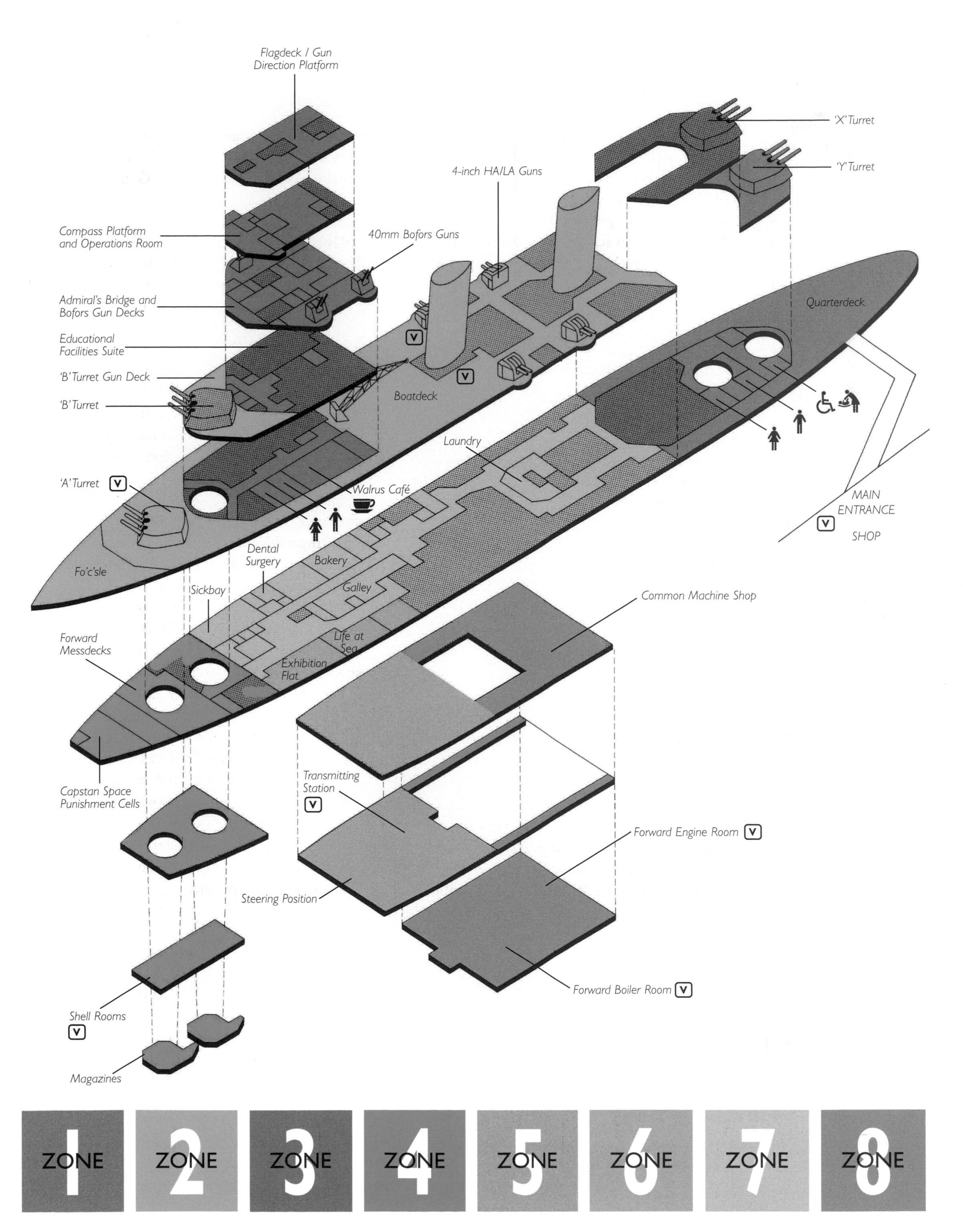

ZONE 1 | ZONE 2 | ZONE 3 | ZONE 4 | ZONE 5 | ZONE 6 | ZONE 7 | ZONE 8

TOUR OF THE SHIP

Above The silver ship's bell was presented by the citizens of *Belfast* in 1948
Photograph: Glyn Williams

Right The ship's honours board
Photograph: Reeve Photography

The Quarterdeck

Your tour of HMS *Belfast* begins here. Officers and ratings always salute when stepping onto the Quarterdeck of a Royal Naval vessel. It was here that flag officers, captains of ships and others who were entitled to the honour were 'piped' on board and where guards and bands were paraded. The Quarterdeck was 'Officer Country' and ratings were not normally permitted to set foot on it except when on duty or to attend the regular Sunday church services presided over by the Captain of the ship. This tradition of worship is maintained when each November the Quarterdeck is the setting for HMS *Belfast*'s annual Remembrance Day Service.

Above Officers and men gathered on the Quarterdeck of a British cruiser for a church service held at sea during the Second World War
IWM Neg. No. A 11316

The White Ensign is flown here day and night by all Royal Naval vessels at sea, and from 'Colours' (8.00 am in summer, 9.00 am in winter) to sunset when in harbour.

Ship's Battle Honours and Silver Bell

Next to the Quartermaster's Lobby, is the board which lists HMS *Belfast*'s battle honours beneath her crest and the motto *Pro Tanto Quid Retribuamus* (What shall we give in return for so much?), which is also the motto of the city of *Belfast* where the ship was built.

The ship's silver bell was presented by the people of *Belfast* in October 1948. On the inner rim of the bell are the names of those children born to serving officers and sailors and christened on board, when the upturned bell was used as a font. When HMS *Belfast* was in service the original ship's bell, which is not on view, was sounded every half-hour to mark the passing of each watch.

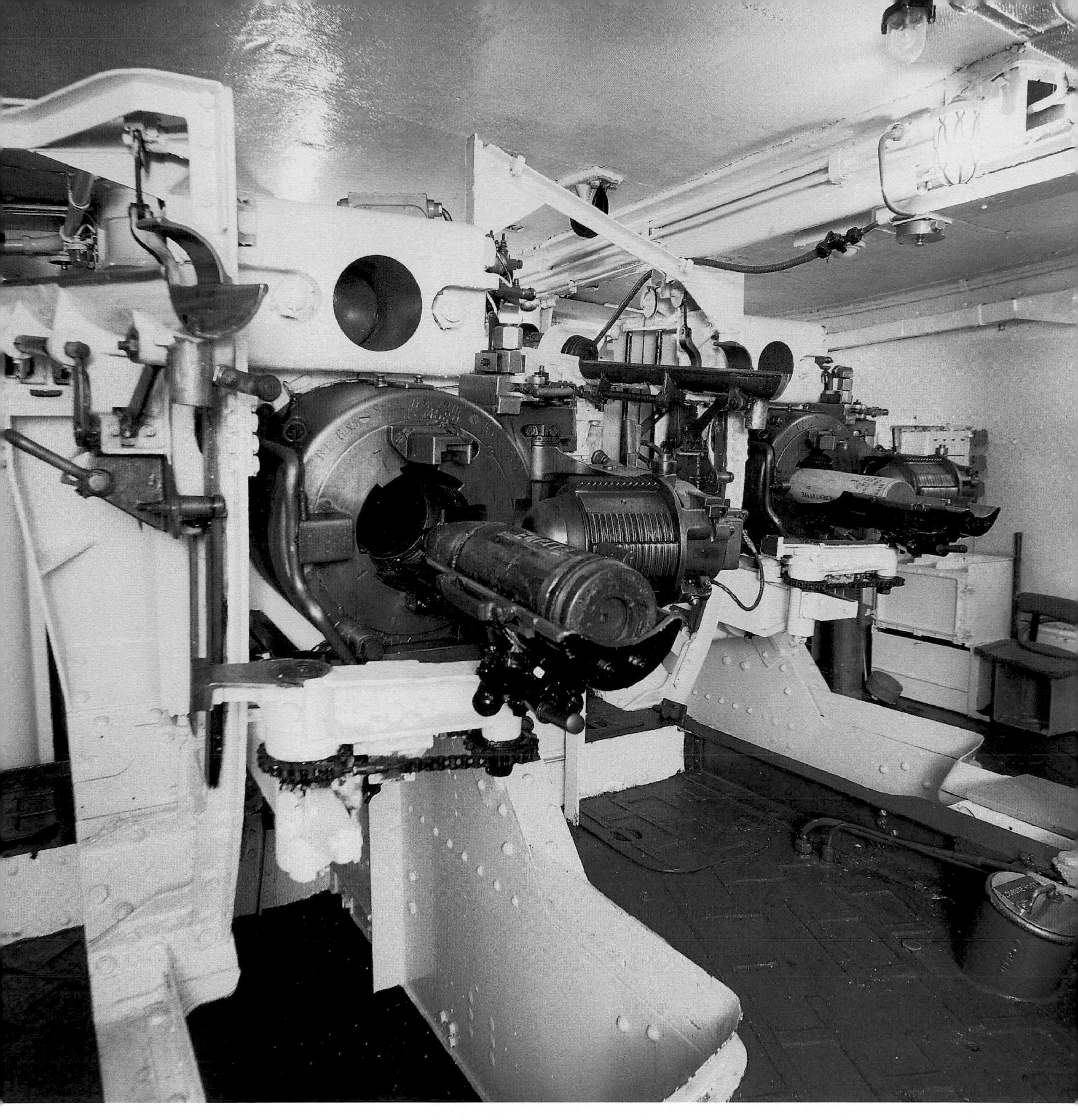

'Y' Turret

Overlooking the Quarterdeck are 'X' and 'Y' Turrets, the after pair of HMS *Belfast*'s four 6-inch Mark XXIII Triple Gun Turrets. 'Y' Turret is open to visitors. Further information about the operation of the ship's 6-inch guns can be found in the section of this guide relating to 'A' Turret, which you will see later on in your tour in Zone 2.

Gunnery Office

In the cabin flat below the after turrets, you can see a young officer dressing for dinner.

Public toilets, including facilities for the disabled and baby changing facilities are located nearby.

Above The interior of 'Y' Turret, showing the shells and cordite charges ready to be rammed into the open breeches of the 6-inch guns

Photograph: Reeve Photography

Access to Zone 2 can be gained from either side of the Quarterdeck. A ramp for disabled visitors is provided on the starboard side of the ship.

4-inch Guns

HMS *Belfast*'s secondary battery of four Twin 4-inch HA/LA Mark XIX Mountings is located in pairs on either side of the ship between her funnels. During the Second World War, HMS *Belfast* carried six of these mountings but the aftermost pair was removed at the end of the war to make way for additional deck-houses. Although they were primarily designed to protect the ship from attack by enemy aircraft, the guns could also be used against surface targets, hence the designation HA/LA - High Angle/ Low Angle.

Below The fixed ammunition shells for HMS *Belfast*'s 4-inch HA/LA mountings weighed 66 pounds (30 kg) and were loaded manually into the breeches of the guns. The shells had to be punched home with a clenched fist as the breech blocks closed automatically and could easily crush the fingers of an open hand. A well-trained gun crew was expected to be able to maintain an average rate of fire of 10 rounds per minute per gun.
IWM Neg. No. A 16317

Two Video Information Monitors on either side of the ship provide further details of the operation of the 4-inch HA/LA mountings.

Top right HMS *Belfast*'s Seaplane Flight, 700 Squadron Fleet Air Arm, pictured in front of one of the ship's Supermarine Walrus Mark I amphibians
IWM Neg. No. HU 447700

Boatdeck and Mainmast

Directly in front of the forward pair of 4-inch mountings lies the great open expanse of HMS *Belfast*'s Boatdeck. When in commission, *Belfast* carried a large number of ship's boats which were hoisted in and out of the water by the 7-ton electric boat crane mounted just aft of the Bridge.

In the early stages of the Second World War, however, the Boatdeck was used as a platform for reconnaissance seaplanes which could be launched by catapult to search for vessels beyond the horizon. After completing a mission, the planes would land in the sea alongside the ship and be lifted back on board by crane. HMS *Belfast* normally carried two seaplanes, each of which was provided with a weather-proof hangar in the wings of the Bridge. Once the ship had been fitted with long-range search radar there was no further need to carry aircraft on board and in mid-1943 the seaplanes were removed. You can find out more about the operation of HMS *Belfast*'s aircraft by watching either of the Video Information Monitors located next to the 4-inch HA/LA mountings.

On leaving the Boatdeck, you should proceed along the port side of the Bridge towards the bow of the ship and HMS *Belfast*'s Forecastle and forward 6-inch Turrets.

Fo'c'sle and Anchors

The Forecastle, or Fo'c'sle, was originally a raised platform on wooden warships where fighting men would gather to rain down fire upon the decks of enemy ships below. In more recent times the Fo'c'sle has been used primarily for the operation of ships' anchors. HMS *Belfast* originally carried three anchors, two on the starboard bow and one on the port. One of the starboard anchors (the sheet anchor) was removed in 1940 and now only the port anchor (weighing 5.5 tons) can be seen stowed on the deck. The anchor cables pass around the cable-holders before disappearing into the Cable Locker below, where they can be seen later on in your tour in Zone 4.

HMS *Belfast*'s anchors were usually raised and lowered by electric power but in an emergency large wooden bars could be inserted into the capstan to operate the machinery manually. It took the combined efforts of 144 men to raise the ship's anchors by this method. Today HMS *Belfast* is permanently moored to the river bed but she still rises and falls about 20 feet (6-7 metres) every day as the tides ebb and flood.

In common with all Royal Naval vessels in harbour, HMS *Belfast* flies the Union Flag daily between 'Colours' and sunset from the jack-staff at her bow.

Above HMS *Belfast's* Boatdeck seen from the port side of the Bridge superstructure
Photograph: Glyn Williams

Left The Fo'c'sle, looking aft towards 'A' and 'B' Turrets, with the port anchor in the foreground
Photograph: Glyn Williams

Above HMS *Belfast*'s forward turrets seen from Hays Galleria
Photograph: Glyn Williams

Right Cross-section of a 6-inch Mark XXIII Triple Mounting, illustrating the ammunition supply

Below The range of the ship's 6-inch guns

'A' Turret

Overlooking the Fo'c'sle, are 'A' and 'B' Turrets, the forwardmost of HMS *Belfast*'s four 6-inch Mark XXIII Triple Gun Turrets. 'A' Turret is open to visitors and there is a Video Information Monitor inside which will tell you all about the complex operation of the ship's main armament.

Each of HMS *Belfast*'s heavily armoured turrets weighs 175 tons and had a crew of 27 working in the turret gun house. A further 22 men worked in the Shell Rooms and Magazines located beneath each turret. The shells and the cordite charges which propelled them were sent up to the gun house by mechanical hoists, where they were rammed into the gun breeches by hand. The guns could be used against enemy targets at sea or on land and had a maximum range of approximately 14 miles (22 kilometres).

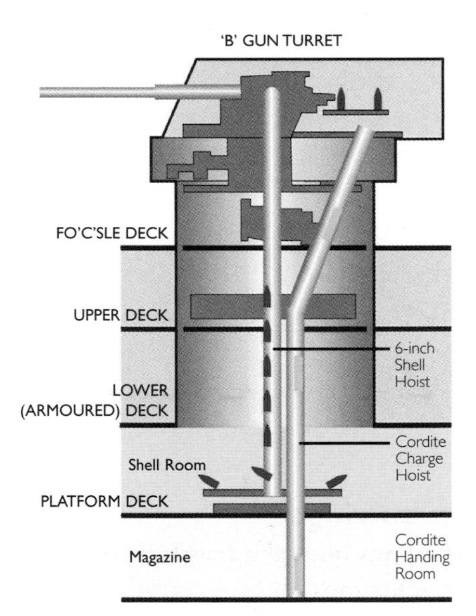

The guns in both forward turrets are trained and elevated onto a target some 12.5 miles (20 kilometres) away in north-west London - the Scratchwood Motorway Services Area on the M1 - a reminder of the awesome power of naval gunnery in the Second World War.

Access to Zone 3 can be gained from 'B' Turret Gun Deck.

Between 1956 and 1959, HMS *Belfast* underwent an extended refit and modernization which resulted in significant alterations to her Bridge superstructure. The original open Bridge was replaced by an enclosed Compass Platform, with a large Operations Room adjacent to it; improved accommodation and command facilities were provided for the Admiral and his staff, and modern close-range anti-aircraft guns were mounted on top of the Bridge wings which had once served as hangars for HMS *Belfast*'s seaplanes. Nevertheless, the essential functions of the Bridge remained largely unchanged, with only the introduction of more sophisticated electronic equipment to mark the passage of time between the last years of HMS *Belfast*'s active life and her days of front-line service in the Second World War.

Admiral's Bridge

HMS *Belfast* was built as a flagship and carried an Admiral for most of her operational life. This additional bridge was provided so that the Admiral and his staff could exercise control over the fleet or squadron of vessels under his command without overcrowding the Compass Platform and interfering with the operation of the ship.

40mm Bofors Guns and Close Range Blind Fire Directors

On either side of the Bridge wings are two 40 mm Twin Bofors Mark V Mountings. In all, HMS *Belfast* was equipped with six of these mountings during the course of her modernization, the two additional mounts being located on her after superstructure. All four of the Bofors mountings can be trained and elevated by hand, although very young children may need some assistance as each mounting weighs almost 7 tons! Fire from the guns was controlled by two Close Range Blind Fire Directors (CRBFDs), which are best seen from the top of the Bridge.

You should now re-enter the interior of the Bridge superstructure, pausing to see the Bridge Wireless Office, before continuing your ascent.

Above Rear-Admiral (later Admiral) Sir Robert Burnett, who flew his flag in HMS *Belfast* at the time of the Battle of North Cape
IWM Neg. No. A 12758

Left View from the open bridge of HMS *Sheffield*, one of HMS *Belfast*'s half-sisters, as she fights her way through heavy seas on convoy duty in the North Atlantic in 1943
IWM Neg. No. A 14890

Below Visitors elevating and training one of the 40 mm Bofors guns
IWM Neg. No. MH 34013

Bridge Wireless Office

On the same level as the Bridge wings, you can see the Bridge Wireless Office (BWO), where all incoming radio messages were received and outgoing messages transmitted. The BWO is still used today by the Royal Naval Amateur Radio Society and enthusiasts can contact them in HMS *Belfast* by using the ship's international call sign, GB2RN. The Electronic Warfare Office, which housed equipment designed to confuse enemy radar and radio signals, is located next to the BWO.

Please mind your head when using the ladders outside the BWO to continue your ascent to the top of the Bridge. Here you will find the Flag Deck, Gunnery Direction Platform and, overlooking them, the Foremast and Forward Director Control Tower.

Flag Deck and Foremast

The Flag Deck was used to send visual signals to nearby vessels. The 10-inch and 20-inch signalling projectors on either side of the deck flashed messages in Morse code and the

Above The Flag Deck was controlled by the Yeoman of Signals, who would pass messages to other vessels in sight using flags, semaphore or Morse code on a signal projector. In this picture, taken on board HMS *Sheffield* in 1941, ice is forming on the projector making the signalman's task extremely difficult.
IWM Neg. No. A 6872

Right The Operations Room as it might have appeared during the Battle of North Cape. The sailors are wearing cotton anti-flash hoods and gloves to protect their faces and hands from the severe burns which could be caused by an enemy shell exploding on the Bridge.
Photograph: Reeve Photography

Foremast was used to hoist communications by flags. HMS *Belfast* was originally equipped with lightweight tripod masts but these were replaced by much stronger lattice masts in order to support the weight of the radar systems fitted to the ship after modernization.

Forward Director Control Tower

The Forward Director Control Tower (DCT) controlled the operation of all four of HMS *Belfast*'s 6-inch Gun Turrets. Originally, the DCT was fitted with a large optical range-finder, but from 1942 onwards targets were normally acquired and tracked by radar.

A second DCT, mounted on the after superstructure, was provided to control the independent operation of the two after Turrets.

Gun Direction Platform

In good visibility, all of HMS *Belfast*'s guns could be controlled from the Gun Direction Platform (GDP) at the forward end of the upper bridge. The Captain's sight on the centre platform was used to indicate targets to the Director Control Tower and the GDP offered an unrivalled vantage point for lookouts manning the four circular sights to search the sea and sky with their binoculars.

You should now begin your descent to the lower levels of the Bridge using the ladder immediately in front of the Director Control Tower. Please mind your head.

Operations Room and Compass Platform

On the deck below are HMS *Belfast*'s Operations Room and Compass Platform, the nerve centre and brain of the entire ship. Although the layout and equipment in both these areas differs from that fitted in the Second World War, the plots and 'state boards' have been reconstructed to show HMS *Belfast*'s role in the Battle of North Cape on 26 December 1943, which ended with the sinking of the German battle-cruiser *Scharnhorst*. You can also hear a sound effect which reconstructs key moments during the course of the battle, wherever possible using original Admiralty signals and drawing upon the recollections of members of HMS *Belfast*'s crew who took part in the engagement.

Above The entire operation of the ship could be controlled from the Compass Platform by the Officer of the Watch. The Captain would usually take command when the ship was in action or carrying out dangerous manoeuvres.
Photograph: Glyn Williams

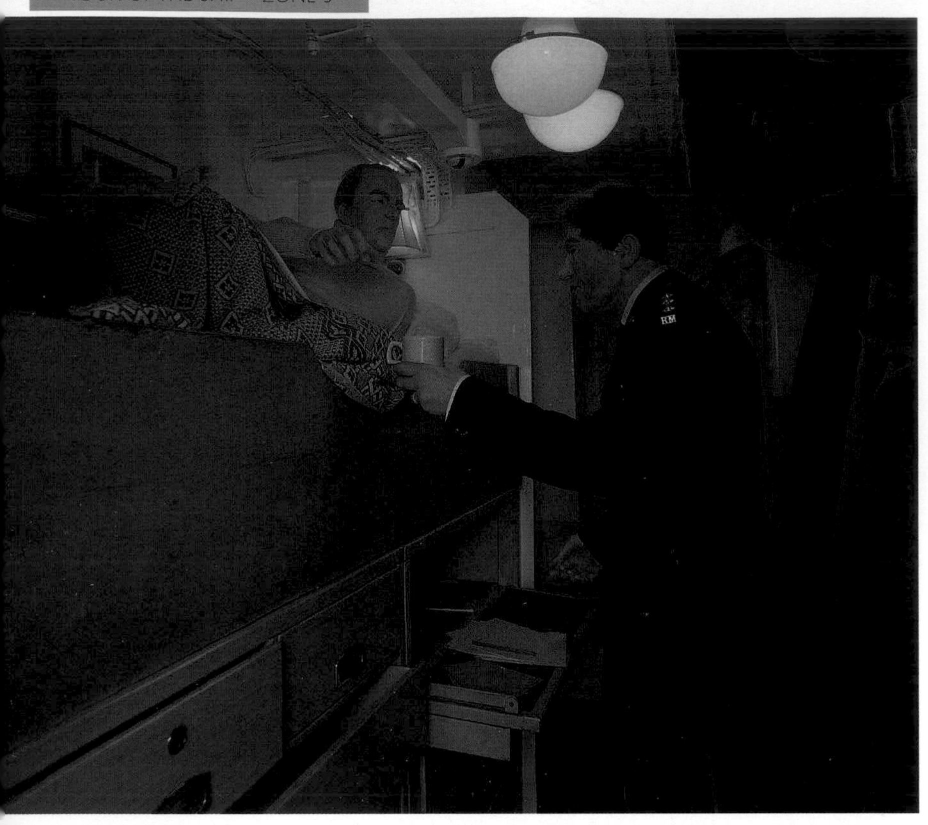

Above A typical sea cabin. The officer handing a mug of scalding hot naval cocoa (known as 'Ki') to his colleague is a Captain of the Royal Marines. The red lighting - 'darken ship routine' - is intended to preserve the crew's night vision when in action and to ensure that HMS *Belfast* shows no bright lights which might betray her position to the enemy.
Photograph: Reeve Photography

Right The Captain's sea cabin. The figure of the Captain is modelled on Captain (later Admiral Sir Frederick) Parham, who commanded HMS *Belfast* from November 1942 to July 1944.
Photograph: Reeve Photography

In the Operations Room, information derived from radar, sonar and intelligence reports on Allied and enemy surface, submarine and air forces was collated and displayed on plots and 'stateboards'. From this combined information, the Captain was able to evaluate the tactical situation and respond accordingly.

It was from the Compass Platform that the Captain or Officer of the Watch controlled the ship at sea, passing steering and engine orders to the helmsman at the wheel in the Forward Steering Position, located six decks below in Zone 6. The ship's course was plotted by the Navigating Officer and his assistants in the Charthouse at the back of the Compass Platform.

Officers' Sea Cabins

On the deck below the Compass Platform are the sea cabins reserved for the Admiral and his staff and for the Captain. These were provided in additions to their day cabins, located beneath the Quarterdeck, so that they could work and sleep in close proximity to the Admiral's Bridge and Compass Platform when the ship was in action or taking part in exercises. There are additional sea cabins for less senior officers on the deck below.

You should now descend to the lowest level of the Bridge, where you will find the ship's cafeteria, the Walrus Café, as well as Ladies and Gents toilets. Access to Zone 4 is via a ladder leading down from the forward end of the Bridge superstructure.

You are now standing on HMS *Belfast*'s Upper (No. 2) Deck, the ship's main accommodation deck. Please proceed towards the bow of the ship and the Forward Messdecks.

6-inch Barbettes

As you walk towards the bow, you will be able to see the huge armoured cylinders, known as barbettes, which protected the 6-inch ammunition hoists bringing shells and cordite charges up to 'A' and 'B' Turrets from the Shell Rooms and Magazines below. The sides of the barbettes are composed of 2-inch (51 mm) plates of armour.

Access to the Shell Rooms is via a ladder just aft of 'A' Turret barbette, but it is suggested that you delay your visit until after you have seen all of the messdecks.

Forward Messdecks

When HMS *Belfast* was first commissioned, a sailor's life was in many respects little changed from the days of Nelson. Sailors joined the Navy at 16 and signed initially for a 12-year engagement, starting from the age of 18.

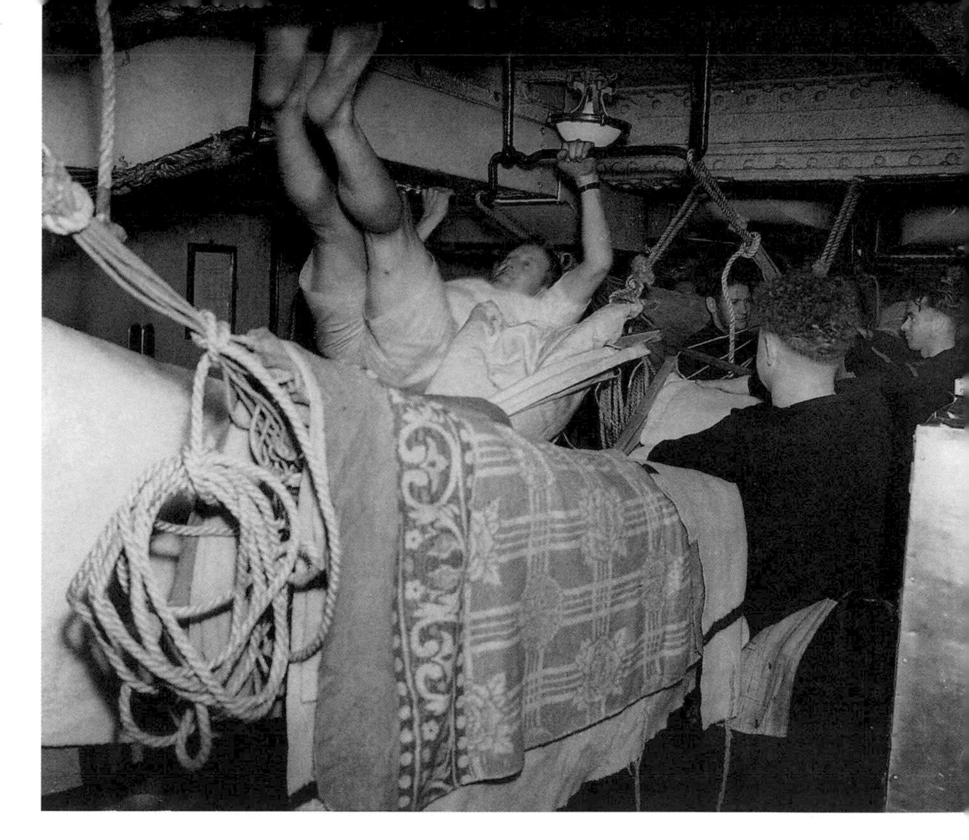

Pay for an Able Seaman was just 21 shillings (£1.05) per week, out of which married men were required to make an allowance of 3 shillings and sixpence (17p) to their wives. A sailor received an additional 12 shillings and sixpence (62p) for each child, and a marriage allowance of 18 shillings (90p) per week was paid direct to his wife while he was at sea. Even allowing for the lower cost of living, the wages of an Able Seaman were barely sufficient to keep his family above the poverty line.

Above A typical messdeck scene during the Second World War, illustrating the art of climbing into a hammock in a confined space
IWM Neg. No. A 2216

Left The Forward Messdecks as they might have appeared when HMS *Belfast* was serving with the Home Fleet in Arctic waters during the Second World War
IWM Neg. No. 96/75/4

Like their predecessors in Nelson's time, HMS *Belfast*'s ratings lived, slept and ate in communal areas known as messes, which were crammed into every available space. While officers were allocated cabins, the ratings slung their hammocks in their mess or slept where they could around the ship. Despite the fact that hammocks were slung only 21 inches

Above Breakfast in a seamen's mess on board the battleship HMS *Rodney* during the Second World War
IWM Neg. No. A 2219

Right One of the ship's punishment cells in rough weather
IWM Neg. No. 96/75/3

(52 cm) apart, the hugely enlarged crews required in wartime (HMS *Belfast*'s authorised peacetime complement of 761 had increased to over 950 by the end of the Second World War) meant that it was not at all unusual for men on different watches to share the use of a hammock or to sleep on the deck beneath one of the mess tables.

Until the 1950s, large warships such as HMS *Belfast* operated a catering system known as Broadside Messing. Each mess would appoint a duty cook who would collect the basic meal for his messmates from the galley, return to his mess, serve it and wash up before returning the empty containers to the galley. Each mess had an allowance to purchase additional or 'luxury' items of food and the ship's supply officer - the 'Pusser' - would present an account for payment at the end of each month. Naval food was stodgy and unimaginative but there was generally plenty of it and many messes preferred to save up their allowance for a first-class binge when they had the opportunity to go on shore.

Capstan Machinery Space and Punishment Cells

The Capstan Machinery Space is situated almost in the bow of the ship and contains the electric motors, gears and vertical shafts which drove the capstans on the Fo'c'sle above (Zone 2). You can see the wooden capstan bars, which were used to turn the capstans by hand in the event of a mechanical breakdown, stowed overhead. Despite this mass of machinery, the compartment was home to 33 sailors, a clear indication of the lack of suitable living space for her crew at the height of HMS *Belfast*'s operational service.

At the forward end of this compartment are the ship's Punishment Cells. The Captain had the power to sentence offenders to periods of up to 14 days' imprisonment for offences such as sleeping on watch, drunkenness or leave-breaking.

On the deck nearby, you can look down through a small access hatch into the Cable Locker where the ship's anchor cables were stowed.

While serving in the North Atlantic during the Second World War, it was not unusual for HMS *Belfast* to encounter hurricane conditions with waves up to 50 feet high. Before leaving the Capstan Machinery Space to visit the Shell Rooms and Magazines, you may like to pause for a moment and imagine what it must have been like to live in this compartment as HMS *Belfast* struggled to lift her bow from beneath the great masses of water foaming over her Fo'c'sle before plunging down to meet the shock of yet another mountainous wave.

Above Interior of 'B' Turret Shell Room, showing the 6-inch projectiles lined up on the handling carousel which revolved around the mechanical hoists leading to the gun house above
Photograph: Reeve Photography

Shell Rooms and Magazines

Please use the ladders leading down from just behind 'A' Turret barbette to enter the Shell Rooms and Magazines, which are located well below the ship's waterline and are the most heavily protected of all the ship's compartments. As well as the vertical protection against shell-fire provided by the main armour belt, 4.5 inches (114 mm) thick, the deck immediately above the Shell Rooms is also armoured to a thickness of 3 inches (76 mm) to provide protection against aerial bombs.

Each of the 6-inch Gun Turrets is served by its own Shell Room and Magazine, with the Magazines and their vulnerable cordite charges sited below the Shell Rooms on the Hold Deck, the lowest of all HMS *Belfast*'s seven habitable decks. The shells and cordite charges were sent up to the turrets above by mechanical hoists.

Above Rum was a regular part of the Royal Navy's diet from the capture of Jamaica in 1655. Originally, sailors received no less than half a pint a day of neat spirit, but in 1740 Admiral Edward Vernon introduced the issue of 'grog' (two parts water to one part rum) which remained one of the great traditions of naval life until as late as 1970.
Photograph: Reeve Photography

Although access to the Magazines and their enclosed Handing Rooms is not permitted for reasons of safety, you can look down into their confined interiors through two hatches, one in each Shell Room. In the event of HMS *Belfast* receiving a hit which threatened an explosion in the Magazines, the compartments could be rapidly flooded to prevent the loss of the ship. In such circumstances, the men working in the Handing Rooms would have had little chance of escape.

You can find out more about the operation of the Shell Rooms and Magazines by watching the Video Information Monitor located in 'A' Turret Shell Room.

Please use the ladders at the after end of 'B' Turret Shell Room to return to the Upper (No. 2) Deck, where your tour of the ship continues.

Provision Issue Room

As you leave Zone 4 you pass the Provision Issue Room. For many of HMS *Belfast*'s crew this was the most important compartment in the entire ship for it was here that the daily rum ration was measured and prepared for issue in a ritual dating back to the middle of the seventeenth century!

Right 'Up spirits!' The rum ration is issued to each mess
IWM Neg. No. A 1777

Located on the starboard side of the ship, the galleries of the Exhibition Flats on the Upper (No. 2) and Lower (No. 3) Decks illustrate aspects of HMS *Belfast*'s history and the story of the Royal Navy in the twentieth century.

Above One of the ship's original 6-inch gun tompion badges manufactured in the fitting out workshops at Harland and Wolff in Belfast City
Photograph: Glyn Williams

Left German magnetic mine of the type which severely damaged the ship in November 1939 on display in the exhibition HMS *Belfast* in War and Peace
IWM Neg. No. 96/75/7

HMS *Belfast* in War and Peace

This major exhibition tells the story of the ship from her inception in the late 1930s to the decision to save her for the nation in 1971. Using original artefacts, documents, plans and drawings as well as contemporary paintings and photographs, ship models and audio-visual displays, HMS *Belfast* in War and Peace provides a comprehensive account of this great historic warship and of the men who served in her.

Life at Sea

The exhibition concentrates on the lives and experiences of the ship's companies during her various commissions. Extensive use has been made of eyewitness accounts and sound recordings.

The direction signs will take you down to the Platform (No. 4) Deck amidships. This area, located well below the waterline and protected by two inches (51 mm) of horizontal armour, houses some of the most important compartments in the ship.

Above This very rare photograph of Royal Marines manning a Transmitting Station in action was taken on board the aircraft carrier HMS *Victorious* during the Second World War
IWM Neg. No. A 7640

6-inch Transmitting Station

The Transmitting Station (TS) was a vital component in the complex system which controlled the operation of HMS *Belfast*'s main armament. In the middle of the compartment, surrounded by its associated radar displays, is the Admiralty Fire Control Table (AFCT), a mechanical computer designed in the 1930s. Information provided by the Forward Director Control Tower on the Bridge (Zone 3) about the range and bearing of an enemy ship was fed into the AFCT, which then calculated the correct angles of train and elevation required for the guns in all four turrets to hit their target.

A smaller version of the AFCT, known as the Admiralty Fire Control Clock (AFCC), is located next door and provided similar data for the after turrets only.

More detailed information about the operation of HMS *Belfast*'s Main Armament Fire Control system is provided by the Video Information Monitor located in the middle of the Transmitting Station.

Forward Conversion Machinery Room

HMS *Belfast* used both direct (DC) and alternating (AC) electric current to power her equipment. The AC current, which supplied her gyro compass, gunnery control systems, radar and wireless equipment, was converted in this compartment and distributed from the switchboard on the other side of the 6-inch Transmitting Station.

Forward Gyro Compass Room

The navigation compass in this compartment worked on the gyroscopic principle which ensured that, whichever way the ship turned, the compass always pointed towards true north. This allowed the ship to be steered accurately and also provided the directional basis for aligning the radars and the gunnery control systems.

Beneath the nearby Soap and Tobacco Store a German magnetic mine exploded on 21 November 1939, almost causing the loss of the ship.

Above HMS *Belfast*'s Forward Steering Position. A secondary emergency steering position was located near the Tiller Flat at the stern of the ship.
Photograph: Glyn Williams

Forward Steering Position

HMS *Belfast* was steered from this heavily protected compartment by the ship's helmsman, who received his instructions from the Officer of the Watch on the Compass Platform (Zone 3). The steering motors and the massive hydraulic rams which operated the ship's rudder are located beneath the Quarterdeck in the Tiller Flat.

The ship's telephone exchange can be seen at the back of the compartment.

Please use the ladders outside the Forward Steering Position to return to HMS *Belfast*'s Upper (No. 2) Deck and Zone 7.

During the course of her extended refit and modernization in the late 1950s, substantial changes were made to the layout of HMS *Belfast*'s Upper (No. 2) Deck amidships, in an attempt to improve the living conditions of her crew in the post-war era. In Zone 7 you can see how HMS *Belfast* looked near the end of her active life, when she was serving mainly in the Far East.

NAAFI Canteen

Since 1921, the Navy Army and Air Force Institute's (NAAFI) Naval Canteen Service has served the Royal Navy both ashore and afloat. Large warships such as HMS *Belfast* were equipped with well-stocked canteens selling a wide variety of goods, including duty-free tobacco, confectionery and small luxury items, as well as essentials such as toothpaste and shoe polish. Wine and spirits were not permitted, but, from 1960 onwards, each member of the crew could purchase up to two cans of beer a day, provided the cans were opened immediately to prevent hoarding. A percentage of the profits generated from this enterprise went towards a general ship's fund, known as the canteen fund, administered by a committee for the benefit of the whole crew.

Right The NAAFI Canteen sold a wide variety of goods. It was usually busy one day in each fortnight - pay day!
Photograph: Reeve Photography

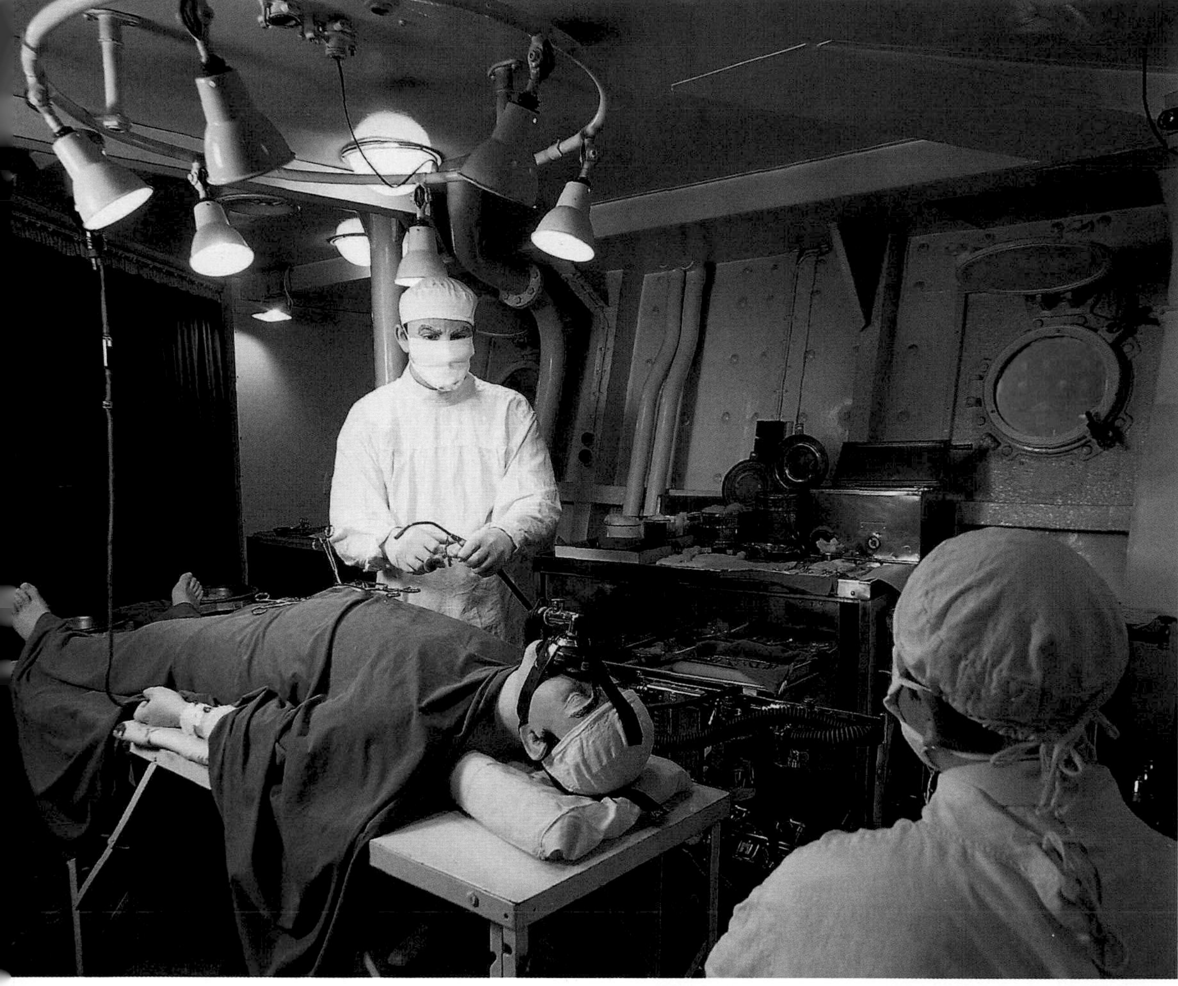

Left The Surgeon Commander carries out an emergency operation in the ship's operating theatre
Photograph: Reeve Photography

Below The Dental Officer was usually a Surgeon Lieutenant Commander and was an important member of the ship's general medical team, but his main task was to look after the dental health of the ship's company
Photograph: Reeve Photography

Sickbay and Dental Surgery

As a cruiser, HMS *Belfast* was specifically designed to spend lengthy periods at sea, so it was essential that she should be adequately equipped to look after the health of her crew. In addition, she was expected to provide emergency services for smaller vessels, such as frigates and destroyers, which lacked all but the most rudimentary medical facilities.

Following modernization, HMS *Belfast* was authorised to carry a medical complement of two officers and up to five sick-berth attendants, including a radiographer and physiotherapist. The operating theatre was sufficiently well equipped, with its own small X-ray machine, for the Surgeon Commander to perform most routine operations but it was normally only used in emergencies because of the movement and vibration of the ship. No such inhibitions seem to have affected the work of his deputy, the Dental Officer!

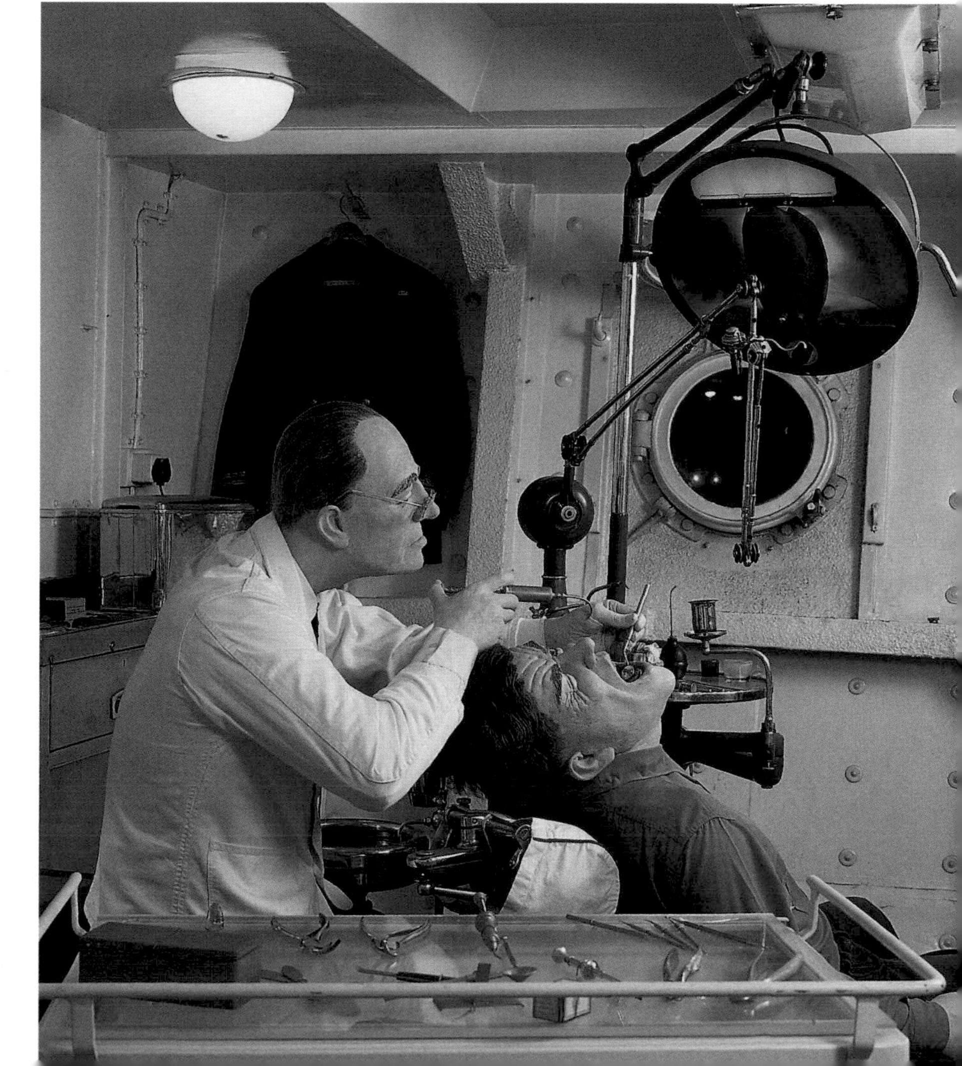

Top Broadside Messing. After collecting the dinner for his mess from the galley, a Royal Marine duty mess cook ladles out his mates' portions at the communal table.
IWM Neg. No. A 16299

Below General Messing. Cafeteria-style service was introduced during the later stages of the Second World War when the Royal Navy took delivery of large numbers of warships designed and built in the United States. This photograph, taken on board the American-built escort carrier HMS *Tracker* in late 1943, illustrates one of the earliest examples of General Messing in a British warship.
IWM Neg. No. A 19771

Ship's Company Galley and Post-war Chief Petty Officers' Messdeck

The Ship's Company Galley dates from the period after HMS *Belfast* 's modernization, when meals for the crew were prepared by properly trained and qualified staff and served from the counter - a practice known as General or Cafeteria Messing. This system brought about a great improvement in the quality and variety of meals served in HM warships and reflected the much better living conditions which were expected by sailors in the post-war navy.

Instead of taking their meals in their mess, the crew now ate in a common canteen - the Ship's Company Dining Hall. The galley staff were supplemented by ratings from each department of the ship, who were detailed to work in the Vegetable Preparation Room.

Additional galleys serving the officers in the Wardroom and the Admiral's Dining Room were located further aft.

On the starboard side of the ship, immediately opposite the Galley, is a typical example of the accommodation provided for HMS *Belfast*'s crew after modernization.

Bakery, Potato Store and Beef Screen

Just aft of the Chief Petty Officers' Messdeck, are a number of compartments devoted to the provisioning of the ship in her last years of active service.

Stowage space in many of the ships which sailed in company with HMS *Belfast* during her service as flagship in the Far East was extremely limited, and she was constantly expected to act as 'mother' to her smaller charges, providing them with essential foodstuffs from her capacious stores. So each day a staff of six bakers had the mammoth task of producing sufficient bread, not only for HMS *Belfast*'s crew, but also for the crews of smaller vessels which had no means of baking bread.

In the darkened Potato Store next door, you can see one of the ship's cats at work!

The Beef Screen served as the ship's butcher's shop. HMS *Belfast* was authorised to carry two trained Royal Marine butchers, who also kept an eye on the refrigerated Galley Ready Use Store.

Entrance to Zone 8

Although Zone 7 continues all the way through to the ship's Quarterdeck and main exit, you may wish to make a detour at this point in order to visit HMS *Belfast*'s Forward Boiler and Engine Rooms. Access to Zone 8 is via a hatchway next to the small Lending Library, at the after end of the Ship's Company Galley.

Above One of HMS *Belfast*'s Royal Marine butchers at work in the Beef Screen
Photograph: Reeve Photography

Above left Ship's cat at work
Photograph: Reeve Photography

Left While church services for the entire ship's company were generally held on the Quarterdeck, this small Chapel was available for private prayer and could be used by men of all religious faiths
Photograph: Reeve Photography

SRE, Chapel and Mailroom

HMS *Belfast*'s Sound Reproduction Equipment Room (SRE) was used at the end of her active life to entertain her crew with popular music and radio programmes.

By tradition, all large Royal Navy warships have an area set aside as a chapel. The ship's Chaplain was an important member of the crew, acting as a friend and

Above The ship's Mail Room
Photograph: Reeve Photography

adviser to sailors of all religious denominations. HMS *Belfast*'s Chapel is still occasionally used for christenings and for private worship.

Next door to the Chapel you can see the ship's Mail Room.

Top right One of HMS *Belfast*'s volunteer Chinese stewards at work in the ship's Laundry
IWM Neg. No. 96/75/2

Ship's Laundry and 21-inch Torpedo

Throughout most of her active life, HMS *Belfast*'s crew were expected to wash their own clothes in buckets and basins, and it was not until her extended refit and modernization in the late 1950s that a well-equipped laundry was finally installed. When the ship was in the Far East, locally recruited Chinese were often employed as laundrymen and, by tragic irony, one of these unfortunate volunteers was killed and four wounded when HMS *Belfast* was struck by shells from a Communist shore battery during the Korean War.

Bottom right A 21-inch Mark IX torpedo being fired from one of the ship's triple torpedo mountings during sea trials in 1939
IWM Neg. No. HU 16022

On the starboard side of the ship, next to the Laundry, you can see an example of a 21-inch Mark IX Torpedo. HMS *Belfast* originally carried six of these weapons in two triple revolving mounts, sited between her funnels, just a bit further forward from where you are now standing. The torpedo mountings were removed and their firing ports plated over during her 1950s' refit.

ZONE 8

HMS *Belfast*'s main propulsive machinery is laid out according to a system first introduced by the United States Navy, known as Unit Propulsion. This system was based upon the grouping together of the boilers and engines into self-contained units – in HMS *Belfast*'s case, four boilers and four engines arranged in pairs (Boiler Room/Engine Room, Boiler Room/Engine Room), in four separate but cross-connected watertight compartments – so that a single hit from an enemy shell or torpedo could never disable more than 50% of the ship's power plant. HMS *Belfast*'s after pair of Boiler and Engine Rooms is closed for reasons of safety but the Forward Boiler and Engine Rooms have been restored and are permanently open to visitors.

Each compartment contains two Video Information Monitors which explain the operation of HMS *Belfast*'s Boilers and Engines in more detail. Access to Zone 8 is via a massive hatchway in the main armoured deck, 2 inches (51 mm) thick, at the after end of the Ship's Company Galley.

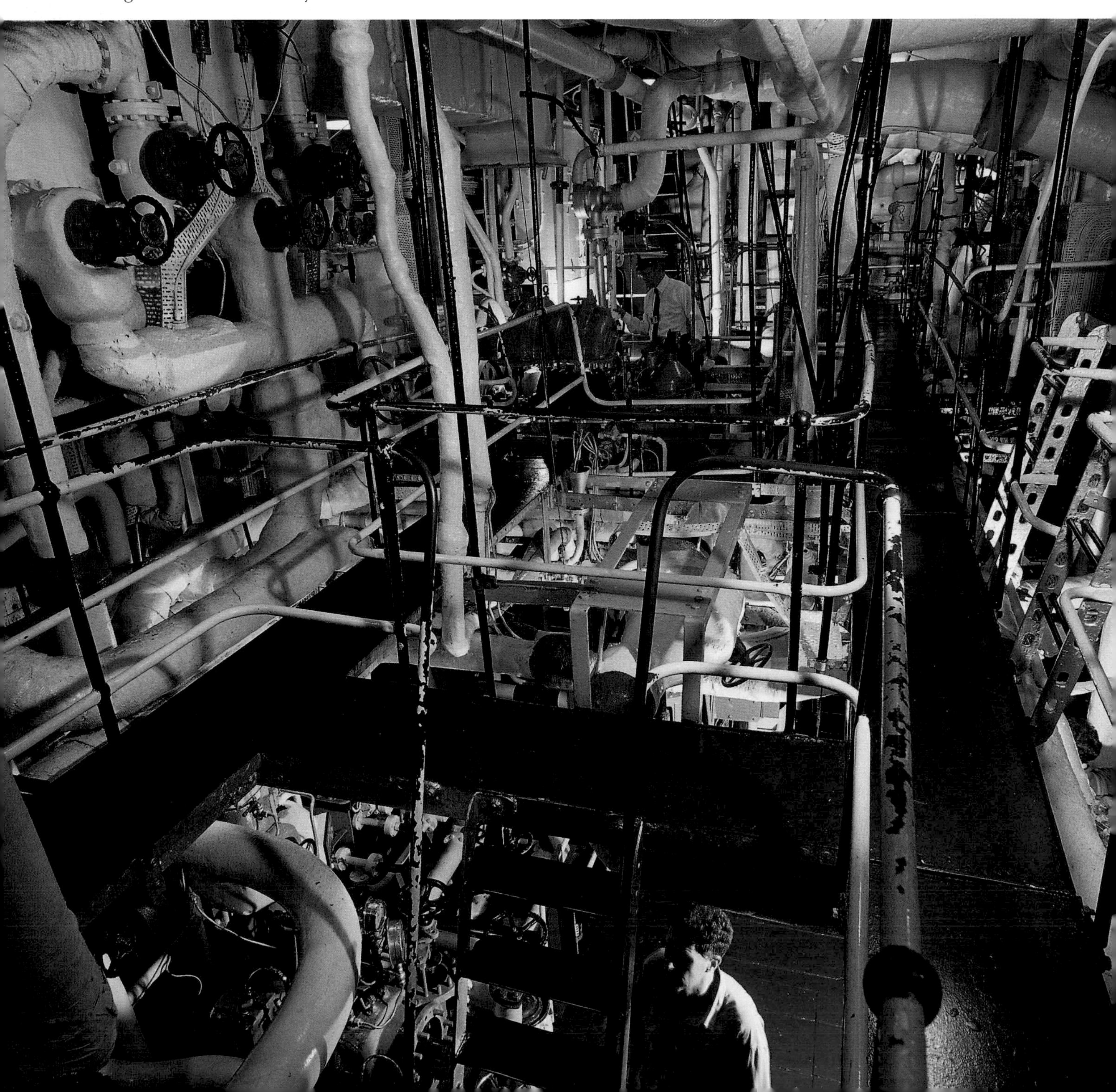

Below Although the Forward Boiler Room, seen here, was kept surprisingly cool by efficient forced draught ventilation, the noise was deafening and the smell of fuel oil in the bilges could be nauseating to the inexperienced
Photograph: Glyn Williams

Forward Boiler Room

The entrance to the Forward Boiler Room is guarded by a double set of doors forming an airlock into the huge compartment beyond.

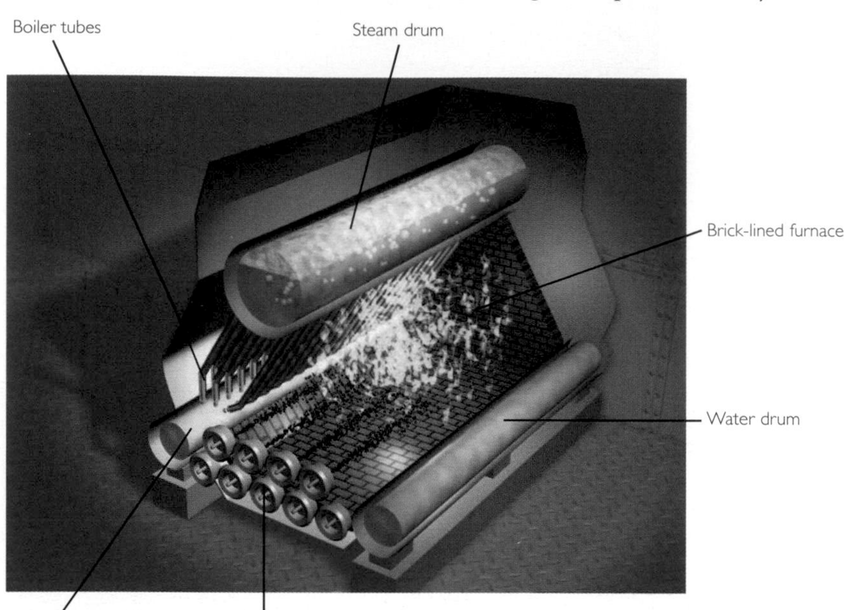

Above Simplified diagram of a ship's boiler, showing how the Furnace Fuel Oil was sprayed into the furnace and how the steam formed in the boiler tubes was collected in the top of the steam drum

Above right A boiler room in the battleship HMS *Prince of Wales* in 1941
IWM Neg. No. A 3912

Below right The oil fuel burners seen here pumped heated Furnace Fuel Oil into the furnace of the boiler in a fine spray. At full speed, HMS *Belfast's* boilers consumed up to 26 tons of fuel per hour.
Photograph: Glyn Williams

This was essential as any sudden change in air pressure could result in the boilers 'flashing back' and incinerating anything, or anyone, in front of them. Once through these doors, you can descend through a maze of pipework and trunking to the floor of the Boiler Room, three decks below. Please be careful when negotiating the ladders in this compartment.

HMS *Belfast's* boilers burned a heavy oil mixture, known as Furnace Fuel Oil (FFO), to produce super-heated steam at a pressure of 350 pounds per square inch. The steam was then piped through to the turbine engines, which in turn drove the propeller shafts. It took about four hours to raise sufficient steam to get the ship under way.

Each boiler consisted of three drums; the two lower drums contained water, which was passed through the furnace in steel tubes. The steam generated was collected in the third drum on the top of the boiler. The front cover of one of the water drums on the port side boiler has been removed so that visitors can look inside.

One of HMS *Belfast's* steam-driven turbo-generators, which provided electric power for the ship when she was at sea, can be seen on the middle level of the Boiler Room, with its turbine and gearbox covers lifted for inspection. Other auxiliary machinery in this compartment includes the fire and bilge pump which drew sea water into the ship's fire mains and pumped out the bilge beneath the machinery.

Please leave the Forward Boiler Room by the ladders leading up on the starboard side of the compartment - not the ladders you used to enter - to reach a winding passageway leading to the Forward Engine Room.

Ship's Company Washrooms

On your way to the Forward Engine Room, you pass by the washrooms and showers provided for the use of HMS *Belfast's* crew as well as an emergency exit leading back up to the Upper (No. 2) Deck and Zone 7.

Forward Engine Room

HMS *Belfast* has four propeller shafts, the two outer ones driven by the engines in the Forward Engine Room and the inner ones driven by the engines in the After Engine Room. Each of the four turbine engines is capable of generating 20,000 shaft horsepower, making a total of 80,000 shp (an average family car develops 100 hp), enough to drive HMS *Belfast* through the water at 32 knots - 36 mph (58 kph).

Each engine has four distinct turbine rotors: the two large high and low pressure turbines, which worked in series to develop full power ahead; a small cruising turbine for more economical speeds; and an astern turbine. The super-heated steam from the boilers could be directed to the desired combination of rotors by means of control throttles, driving the turbines, which in turn drove the propeller shafts through the gearbox mechanism attached to each engine.

The auxiliary machinery in this compartment includes a steam-powered turbo-generator and a set of twin evaporators, which were used to distil sea water for the boilers and for domestic purposes.

Above The Forward Engine Room, illustrating the operation of the control throttles which directed steam to the starboard engine
Photograph: Glyn Williams

Right The housings have been raised to enable visitors to see the insides of the starboard outer engine's massive turbine rotors and gearbox
Photograph: Reeve Photography

Below right Maintenance and repair of the ship's hull and engineering equipment was carried out using the machine tools in the Common Machine Shop
Photograph: Reeve Photography

Please use the ladder at the forward end of the Engine Room, near the control position, to continue your tour.

Common Machine Shop

This workshop supplied the needs of all the ship's technical departments and some of the equipment on view is still used today by the ship's maintenance staff.

On leaving the Common Machine Shop, you emerge once again on HMS *Belfast*'s Upper (No. 2) Deck at the after end of Zone 7. The main exit taking you back onto the Quarterdeck is signposted to your left.

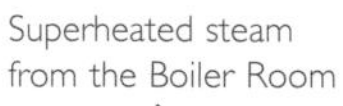

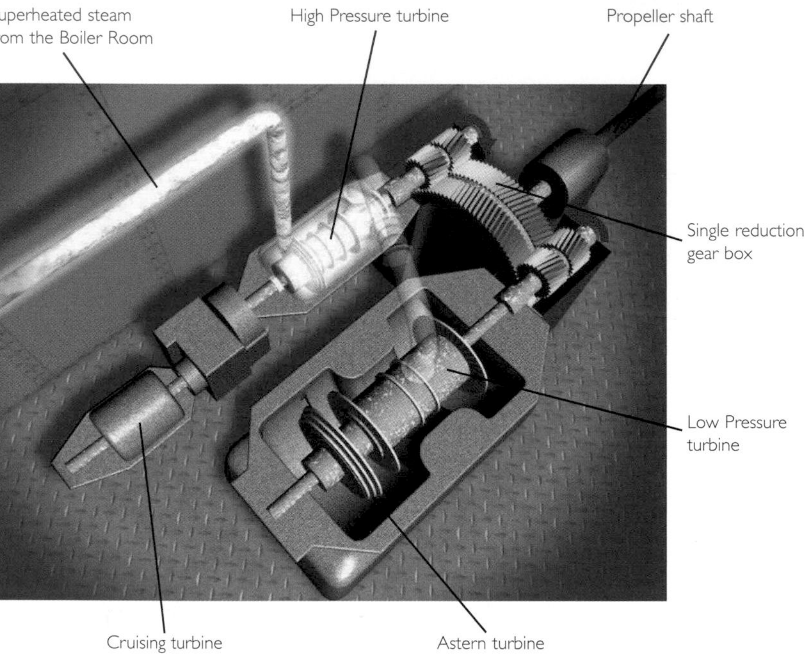

Above Simplified diagram of a ship's engine, illustrating the arrangement of the turbines and the High and Low Pressure turbines working in series

You are now at the end of your tour of HMS *Belfast*. Please feel free to retrace your steps if you would like to revisit any part of the ship. We hope that you have thoroughly enjoyed your visit to this historic warship.

Souvenir shop

You may leave the ship by crossing the gangway to the south bank of the Thames, where you can visit HMS *Belfast*'s souvenir shop.

SHIP SPECIFICATIONS

Class
Edinburgh. Modified Southampton class

Sister ship
HMS *Edinburgh* (sunk May 1942)

Built
Harland and Wolff Shipyard, Belfast
Keel laid 10 December 1936

Launched
17 March 1938 – St Patrick's Day

Commissioned into Royal Navy
5 August 1939

Standard displacement
11,553 tons

Overall length
613 feet 6 inches (187 metres)

Beam
69 feet (21 metres)

Draught
19 feet 9 inches (6.1 metres)

Armament (1959)
Twelve (4 x 3) 6-inch
Eight (4 x 2) 4-inch HA/LA
Twelve (6 x 2) 40mm Bofors AA

Propulsive machinery
Four Admiralty 3-drum boilers; four steam powered Parsons single reduction geared turbines driving four shafts at 80,000 shaft horsepower

Maximum speed
32 knots (36 miles / 58 km per hour)

Complement
750 – 850 (as flagship)

Above External profile and transverse sections of HMS *Belfast* in 1942

Below External profile and deck plan of HMS *Belfast* after her extended refit in 1962

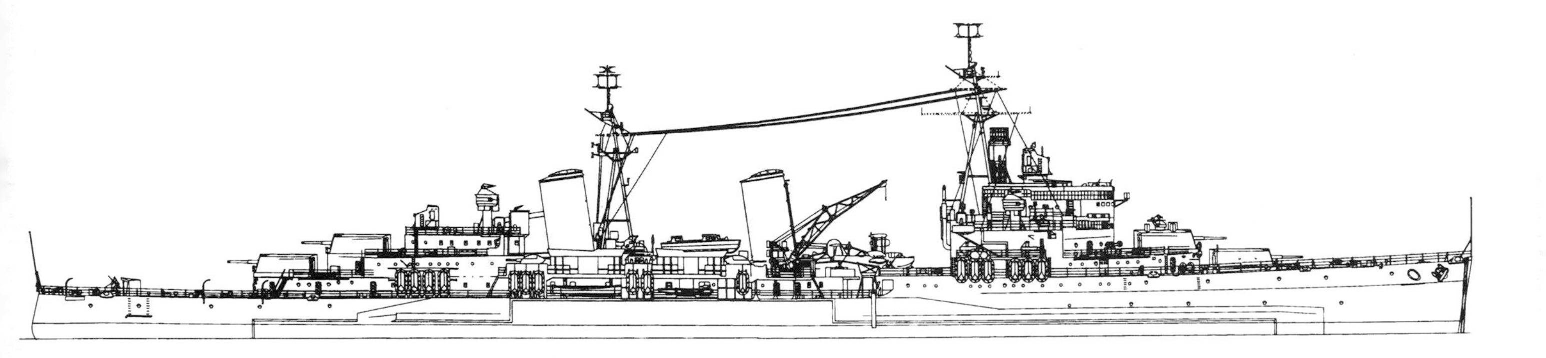

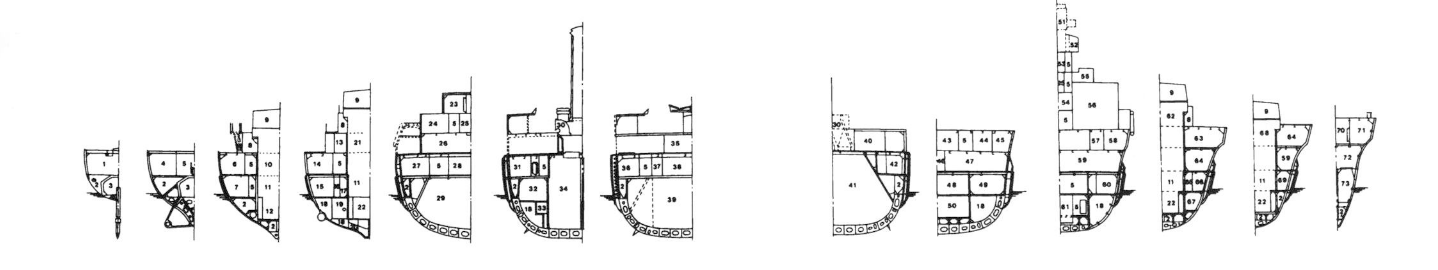

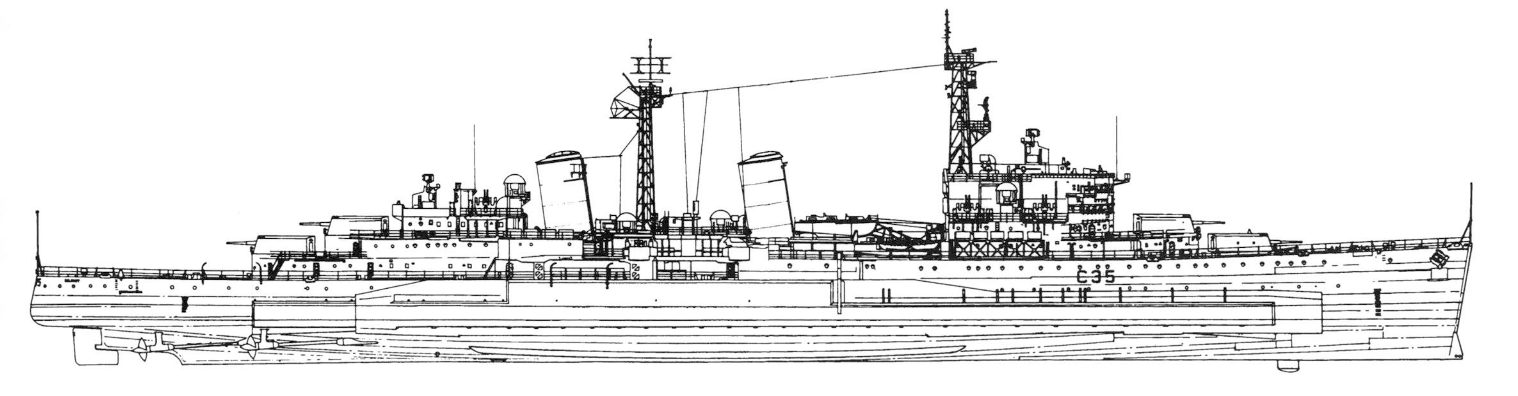

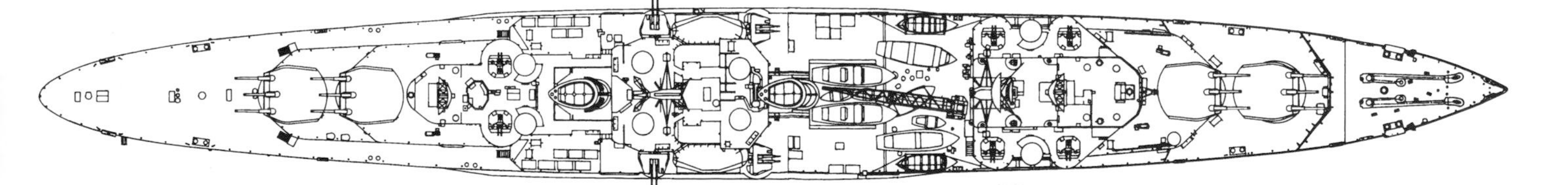

HISTORY OF THE SHIP

Origins and Conception

The term 'cruiser' dates back to the days of sailing ships, when large frigates could be deployed to operate independently against enemy commerce raiders. During the nineteenth century, when sail gave way to steam, and wooden ships were replaced by vessels built of iron, and later of steel, the cruiser evolved into a powerful warship which was used to patrol the British Empire's far-flung maritime trade routes.

Above HMS *Southampton* pictured shortly after her completion in March 1937. With a main armament of twelve 6-inch guns and a speed of 32 knots, the 'Southampton' class set the standard for all future classes of large light cruiser built for the Royal Navy.
IWM Neg. No. HU 69048

Right 'I name this ship *Belfast*. May God bless her and all who sail in her.' HMS *Belfast* runs down the slipway to the cheers of shipyard workers and their families.
IWM Neg. No. HU 43755

Above HMS *Belfast* at full speed on the measured mile range off Greenock on 23 May 1939. The 4-inch secondary battery mountings and main armament Director Control Towers have not yet been fitted.
IWM Neg. No. HU 43767

Both before and during the First World War (1914 -1918), cruisers were increasingly required to undertake a wide variety of different tasks, ranging from their traditional role of commerce protection to direct support of the Navy's battleships. In the aftermath of the Washington Naval Treaty of 1922, which imposed restrictions upon the size and armament of all types of warship, British cruiser construction had settled down to produce two distinct types of vessel:- 'heavy cruisers' with 8- inch guns and displacements of up to 10,000 tons, whose size and great range made them particularly suitable for long-range deployment in defence of trade, and smaller 'light cruisers' with 6-inch guns, for more offensive deployment in support of the battle fleet.

In the mid-1930s, however, a new type of vessel emerged, which combined the size advantage of the earlier generation of heavy cruisers with large numbers of rapid firing 6- inch guns. These large light cruisers were built in great numbers and many of them continued in service long after the end of the Second World War.

HMS *Belfast* was one of the most powerful large light cruisers ever built and is now the only surviving vessel of her type to have seen active service during the Second World War.

Design and Construction

In 1936, the Admiralty decided to order two enlarged and improved versions of the large light cruisers of the 'Southampton' class with sixteen 6-inch guns in four quadruple turrets, on a displacement of 10,000 tons, the maximum permitted under the terms of the Washington Treaty. In keeping with the policy of naming the 'Southamptons' after British cities, it was decided to call the two ships '*Edinburgh*' and '*Belfast*'.

In the event, it proved impossible to manufacture effective quadruple 6-inch mountings and the final design specified an improved version of the successful triple mounts used in the 'Southampton' class. The weight saved was used to improve armour protection and to increase the ships' anti-aircraft armament by 50%.

Construction of the second ship of the 'Edinburgh' class was assigned by tender to Messrs Harland and Wolff of Belfast on 21 September 1936 and the vessel was launched by Mrs Neville Chamberlain on St Patrick's Day, 17 March 1938. The Navy Estimates for that year show that her planned cost was £2,141,514, including £75,000 for the guns and £66,500 for aircraft.

After fitting out and builder's trials, HMS *Belfast* was commissioned into the Royal Navy on 5 August 1939 under the command of Captain G A Scott DSO RN.

Below A slight hitch during the formal commissioning ceremony held at sea on 5 August 1939. The ensign has jammed in the ensign staff halliard and a seaman has been sent aloft to release it.
IWM Neg. No. HU 4645

Above The German liner SS *Cap Norte* of the Hamburg Sud-American line, captured by HMS *Belfast* on 9 October 1939
IWM Neg. No. HU 10272

Right HMS *Belfast* shortly after her mining in the Firth of Forth. Members of the ship's company can just be seen getting ready to launch life rafts from the Quarterdeck.
IWM Neg. No. HU 16012

Below A Royal Marine gun crew sleeping in one of HMS *Sheffield's* 6-inch turrets while on patrol in 1941. *Sheffield* was a half-sister to HMS *Belfast* and the two cruisers fought alongside each other at the Battle of North Cape.
IWM Neg. No. A 6879

Early War Service

On the outbreak of war with Germany in September 1939, HMS *Belfast* formed part of the 18th Cruiser Squadron operating out of the Home Fleet's main base at Scapa Flow in Orkney.

Over the course of the next few weeks the ship was constantly on patrol in Northern waters, as part of the Royal Navy's efforts to impose a maritime blockade on Germany. On 9 October, HMS *Belfast* successfully intercepted the German liner SS *Cap Norte* which was trying to return to Germany disguised as a neutral vessel. The liner was boarded and sent under armed guard to a British port. *Cap Norte* was the largest enemy merchant ship intercepted to date and under Admiralty law *Belfast's* crew received 'prize money' in the form of a cash gratuity for her capture.

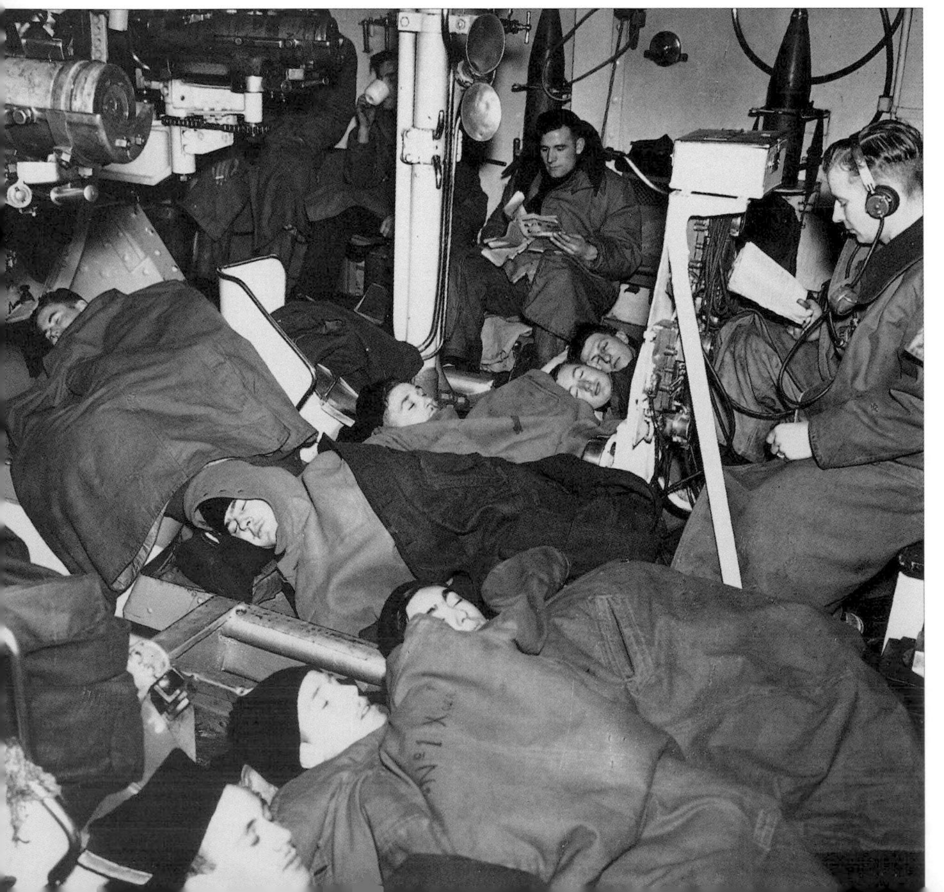

Mined!

The Germans exacted a swift revenge for HMS *Belfast's* early success in capturing the *Cap Norte* when, shortly before 11.00 am on

21 November 1939, whilst leaving the Firth of Forth, she was rocked by the violent detonation of a magnetic mine. Although casualties were mercifully light, the ship's back was broken and the damage to her hull and machinery caused by the whiplash effect of the explosion was so severe that almost three years were to elapse before she could be made fit for action.

Arctic Convoys

When she finally rejoined the Home Fleet in November 1942, under the command of Captain (later Admiral Sir Frederick) Parham, HMS *Belfast* was the largest and arguably the most powerful cruiser in the Royal Navy. Not only had she been 'bulged' amidships, increasing her standard displacement to 11,500 tons and significantly improving her stability, but she had also been equipped with the most up-to-date radar and fire control systems. As a result, she was soon in the forefront of Britain's naval war in the Atlantic; as flagship of the Tenth Cruiser Squadron, responsible for providing close range heavy cover for the Arctic convoys taking supplies to the Soviet Union.

On 21 February 1943, wearing the flag of Rear-Admiral (later Vice-Admiral Sir Robert) Burnett, HMS *Belfast* left Iceland for the Russian port of Murmansk in support of Convoy JW53. Although the Germans failed to prevent the convoy from reaching its destination, hurricane force gales caused severe damage to warships and merchant vessels alike. Apart from occasional offensive sweeps with the battleships and aircraft carriers of the Home Fleet, HMS *Belfast* was to spend most of 1943 engaged on similar duties in the icy waters of the Arctic.

Above HMS *Belfast* moored in Hvalfjord, Iceland, in the spring of 1943. Her Walrus seaplane has just landed alongside.
IWM Neg. No. HU 63915

Below The ammunition ship *Mary Luckenback* explodes during an air attack on the Arctic Convoy PQ 18 in September 1942. Between August 1941 and the end of the war, a total of 75 convoys made the perilous journey to and from north Russia, carrying four million tons of supplies, including 5,000 tanks and 7,000 aircraft for use by Soviet forces fighting against the German Army on the Eastern Front.
IWM Neg. No. A 12271

Above The ice-encrusted 6-inch guns of HMS *Belfast*'s 'A' and 'B' turrets are trained ready for action on either beam during convoy duties in the Arctic in November 1943

IWM Neg. No. A 20687

Right Sailors and Royal Marines pose for the camera during a break from the essential task of clearing ice from HMS *Belfast*'s upper decks. Apart from rendering guns and fire control systems inoperable, an accumulation of ice could make the ship top heavy and seriously affect her stability in the event of damage.

IWM Neg. No. HU 8799

The Battle of North Cape

Between the beginning of November and the middle of December 1943, no less than three eastbound and two westbound Arctic convoys reached their destinations without loss and the Commander-in-Chief of the German Navy, Grand Admiral Doenitz, came under increasing pressure to sanction a sortie by one of

Left Originally intended as lightly armoured 'pocket battleships', *Scharnhorst* and her sister ship *Gneisenau* were redesigned on Hitler's orders with heavy protective armour and a very high top speed. *Scharnhorst's* main armament of nine 28 cm (11-inch) guns was, however, smaller than that normally mounted in a battleship and she was always described by the Royal Navy as a battle cruiser. Able to outrun any existing battleship and outfight any cruiser, she was ideally suited for commerce raiding.
IWM Neg. No. HU 1042

Germany's few remaining heavy surface ships to interrupt the flow of supplies via the Arctic convoy route. On the evening of 25 December, the battle cruiser *Scharnhorst*, her mess decks adorned with traditional Christmas decorations, set sail from Langefjord with five destroyers. Her mission: to attack and destroy Convoys JW 55B and RA55A as they passed the northern tip of Norway.

Unknown to the Germans, British Intelligence was intercepting and decyphering German signals and within hours the Admiralty had informed the Commander-in-Chief Home Fleet, Admiral Fraser, that *Scharnhorst* was at sea, giving him plenty of time to dispose his forces. While Rear-Admiral Burnett in HMS *Belfast*, with the cruisers *Norfolk* and *Sheffield*, screened the convoys and kept *Scharnhorst* in play, Admiral Fraser, in the battleship HMS *Duke of York*, accompanied by the large light cruiser HMS *Jamaica* and four destroyers, would cut her off from the south.

Early on the morning of Boxing Day, 26 December, the *Scharnhorst*, having lost contact with her destroyers, encountered Burnett and his cruisers only to be driven off after being hit by one of HMS *Norfolk*'s 8-inch shells. After a further unsuccessful attempt to break through to the convoys, the *Scharnhorst*

Below HMS *Duke of York* opens fire. The much greater weight of the British battleship's 14-inch shells gave her a significant advantage over *Scharnhorst* in a gunnery duel, especially when firing at long range.
IWM Neg. No. A 7550

retreated at high speed with *Belfast* and *Sheffield* in hot pursuit, driving the enemy towards Admiral Fraser and the 14-inch guns of HMS *Duke of York.* Shortly after gaining radar contact, the *Duke of York* succeeded in hitting the German battle cruiser with her first salvo.

Although *Scharnhorst* twisted and turned, she was unable to shake off her tormentors and eventually her fire slackened sufficiently to allow Admiral Fraser to send in his destroyers. Hit by at least three torpedoes and pounded by heavy artillery at point blank range, the battle cruiser was now dead in the water. Finally, the *Belfast* and *Jamaica* were ordered to sink her with torpedoes. Even as HMS *Belfast* fired, *Scharnhorst*'s radar blip vanished, to be followed by a series of muffled underwater explosions as she slipped beneath the waves. Only thirty-six out of her complement of 1,963 men survived.

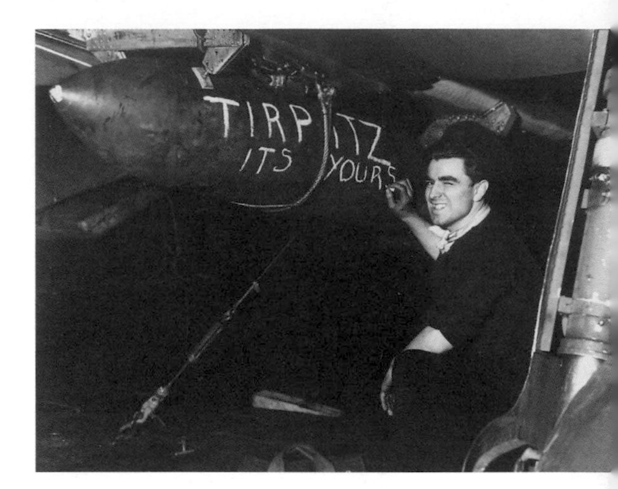

Right 'Bombing-up' a Barracuda prior to the attack on *Tirpitz* on 3 April 1944
IWM Neg. No. A 22640

Operation 'Tungsten'

On 30 March 1944, HMS *Belfast* sailed from Scapa Flow in company with a powerful force of battleships and aircraft carriers. Their objective was the battleship *Tirpitz*, Germany's last surviving heavy surface unit, moored in the supposedly impregnable anchorage of Altenfjord in northern Norway.

Below The battleship *Tirpitz*; a solitary brooding shape amidst the wintry landscape of one of her Norwegian lairs. With a main armament of eight 38 cm (15-inch) guns, *Tirpitz* was one of the most powerful ships in European waters.
IWM Neg. No. HU 50947

In the early hours of 3 April, having approached to within 120 miles of the Norwegian coast, the carriers launched 42 bombers and 80 fighters in the largest air strike yet undertaken by the Fleet Air Arm. *Tirpitz* was hit by 15 bombs and although not sunk, was incapable of putting to sea for several months. She was finally destroyed by heavy bombers from 617 Squadron RAF in November 1944.

Above Barracuda bombers from the fleet carriers *Victorious* and *Furious* flying over Altenfjord during the course of Operation 'Tungsten'
IWM Neg. No. A 22631

Right HMS *Belfast* using her 4-inch secondary battery against German shore positions in Normandy on the night of 27 June 1944
IWM Neg. No. A 24325

D-Day Bombardment

Ever since the disastrous raid upon Dieppe in 1942, when the assaulting troops had been cut down by well-protected German gun positions, Allied amphibious operations had been supported by heavy naval bombardments. Now, for D-Day, the biggest landing of all, the bombardment force comprised 5 battleships, 2 monitors, 20 cruisers and 65 destroyers. But this was only a part of the total force of 2,700 seagoing vessels and 1,900 smaller craft which were deployed in support of Operation 'Neptune', the naval side of the Normandy landings.

This huge armada was divided into two naval task forces and five assault forces, one for each of the main landing beaches. Each of the assault forces was in turn supported by its own naval bombardment force. As flagship of bombardment Force E, HMS *Belfast* was part of the Eastern Naval Task Force, with responsibility for supporting the British and Canadian assaults on 'Gold' and 'Juno' beaches and, at 5.30 am on 6 June 1944, was one of the very first ships to open fire on German positions in Normandy.

Over the course of the next five weeks she was almost continuously in action, firing thousands of rounds from her main 6-inch and secondary 4-inch batteries in support of Allied troops fighting their way inland against skilful and determined German opposition. Her last shoot took place in company with the battleship HMS *Rodney* and the monitor HMS *Roberts* on 8 July, during the course of heavy fighting for the city of Caen. Two days later, the battle lines having moved beyond the range of her 6-inch guns, HMS *Belfast* set sail for Plymouth Devonport and a well-earned refit, prior to being despatched to the Far East. She had fired her guns in anger for the last time in European waters.

Above King George VI takes the salute from the bridge of HMS *Belfast* during a review of the Home Fleet at Scapa Flow on 15 May 1944.
Unknown to her ship's company, both the King and the Prime Minister, Winston Churchill, had made private arrangements to secure a grandstand view of the D-Day landings and had been assigned to HMS *Belfast*. In the event, both VIPs vetoed each other's plans and *Belfast* was allowed to proceed to the Normandy coast unencumbered by her exalted but potentially awkward passengers!
IWM Neg. No. A 23329

Left Rear-Admiral Dalrymple-Hamilton, commanding bombardment Force E, on the bridge of HMS *Belfast* with Captain Parham (smoking a pipe) in the early hours of 6 June 1944
IWM Neg. No. HU 65372

Above Children of British and Commonwealth civilian internees are entertained at a party held on board HMS *Belfast* in Shanghai on 28 September 1945
IWM Neg. No. A 30854

The Far East

Although the dropping of the atomic bombs on Hiroshima and Nagasaki in August 1945 hastened the surrender of Imperial Japan before HMS *Belfast*'s arrival in the Far East, she was still able to perform much useful work in helping to evacuate the emaciated survivors of Japanese prisoner of war and civilian internment camps from China, and until the autumn of 1947 she was fully occupied with peace-keeping duties in the Far East.

Following her first peacetime refit, HMS *Belfast* returned to the Far East in December 1948 as flagship of the Fifth Cruiser Squadron.

By this time, China was in turmoil as the struggle between the Nationalist government and the Chinese Communist Party, led by Mao Zedong, moved towards its conclusion. In April 1949, the British sloop HMS *Amethyst* was disabled and blockaded in the Yangste River by Communist shore batteries. An attempt to rescue the stricken vessel failed with heavy loss of life and the *Amethyst* was trapped in the Yangste for six weeks until she managed to escape on the night of 30 July.

Right HMS *Amethyst* pictured in Hong Kong harbour, following repairs to the damage inflicted by Chinese Communist artillery in the Yangste River
IWM Neg. No. HU 45388

Although HMS *Belfast* was not actively involved in the crisis, the Commander-in-Chief Far Eastern Station, Admiral Sir Patrick Brind, was wearing his flag on board in Hong Kong and all orders given to *Amethyst*'s temporary commander, Lieutenant Commander J S Kerans, emanated from *Belfast*.

The Korean War

At the end of the Second World War, the ancient kingdom of Korea was split between a hard-line Communist regime in the north and a western-style government, supported by the United States, in the south. On 25 June 1950, the North Korean People's Army invaded South Korea. The United Nations Security Council voted to give aid to the South and, after halting the North Koreans around the port of Pusan, UN forces landed behind enemy lines at Inchon and quickly overran most of the country. In October 1950, however, Communist China entered the war and thousands of 'People's Volunteers'- six full armies - crossed into North Korea. UN troops were forced to retreat and by the summer of 1951, both sides had settled down to a lengthy war of attrition along the line of

Above HMS *Belfast* using her forward 6-inch gun turrets to bombard enemy shore positions on the west coast of Korea in 1951. During the course of the Korean War *Belfast* fired so many rounds from her main armament that she had to have all twelve 6-inch barrels replaced.
IWM Neg. No. A 32031

Left Ratings celebrating Christmas in Number 20 Mess on board HMS *Belfast* in 1951. Throughout the Korean War a significant proportion of the ship's company were National Servicemen.
IWM Neg. No. HU 36593

the 38th Parallel. After two years of negotiations, the Korean War came to an end on 27 July 1953.

HMS *Belfast* was amongst the very first British ships to go into action off Korea, bombarding in support of retreating South Korean and American troops only eleven days after the North Korean invasion. Her service in the Korean War, during which she spent no less than 404 days on active patrol, was as long and arduous as that with the Home Fleet during the Second World War.

On 27 September 1952, she sailed for home, having fired her guns in anger for the last time.

Right The grave of Leading Steward Lau So, one of HMS *Belfast*'s Chinese volunteers, who was killed when the ship was hit by a Communist shore battery on 29 July 1952
IWM Neg. No. HU 36644

Below HMS *Belfast* anchored off Plymouth Devonport in July 1959 after her Extended Refit and Modernization.
Her bridge superstructure has been enlarged, modern radar and fire control systems fitted and her anti-aircraft armament brought up to date. In addition, the accommodation for the ship's company has been greatly improved.
IWM Neg. No. A 34201

The Last Years at Sea

By the time HMS *Belfast* returned from Korea, the days of the big gun armoured warship were drawing to a close. But the Royal Navy still needed a small number of cruisers to support its aircraft carriers and to serve as flagships on Foreign Stations. In 1956, HMS *Belfast* was taken in hand at Devonport Dockyard for Extended Refit and Modernization. In August 1959, she set sail once more for the Far East. Almost three years were to elapse before she returned to Home waters.

For her ship's company, *Belfast*'s last years at sea were perhaps the happiest in her eventful life, with ample opportunity for relaxation in between peacetime exercises and a hectic round of official visits to some of the world's most exotic ports. For this was the era of 'the wind of change' which, in a few short years, saw the old British Empire transformed into a Commonwealth of independent nation states.

As Britain said goodbye to its empire, the need for a large peacetime navy dwindled. Even before HMS *Belfast* had completed a circumnavigation of the world via the Pacific Ocean and the Panama Canal in 1962, it was clear that her sea-going days were numbered. In August 1963, following a final exercise in the Mediterranean, she paid off into reserve for the last time before being reclassified as a Harbour Accommodation Ship.

Above Leaving Singapore in April 1962 at the end of her last Far Eastern service commission
IWM Neg. No. HU 4646

Below Alone and forlorn, the old cruiser lies in Fareham Creek, near Portsmouth, awaiting her final journey to the ship breakers
IWM Neg. No. MH 13768

Above Nearly home. With her top-mast just clearing the upper-works of Tower Bridge, HMS *Belfast* arrives in the Pool of London on 15 October 1971.
IWM Neg. No. MH 15061

In Trust for the Nation

In May 1971, after 32 years of service during which she had steamed nearly half a million miles, the last of the Royal Navy's wartime cruisers was 'Reduced to Disposal', in preparation for sale and destruction by the ship breakers.

Fortunately, help was at hand. As early as 1967, the Imperial War Museum had investigated the possibility of preserving a Second World War cruiser but the government of the day had been reluctant to provide the necessary funding. Undeterred, the Museum encouraged the formation of an independent trust led by one of HMS *Belfast*'s former captains, Rear-Admiral Sir Morgan Morgan-Giles. Eventually, this devoted band of enthusiasts succeeded in bringing her to London where she opened to visitors on Trafalgar Day, 21 October 1971.

HMS *Belfast* has been a part of the Imperial War Museum since 1978 and is the first ship to be preserved for the nation since Nelson's *Victory*.

MUSEUM SERVICES

Improving our Service

The Imperial War Museum aims for the highest possible standards of customer service in HMS *Belfast*. Please let the Director know if you have any comments, complaints or suggestions for improvement.

Opening Hours

Open every day except 24 - 26 December
Summer (1 March - 31 October)
Open 10.00 am to 6.00 pm
with last admissions at 5.15 pm

Winter (1 November - 28 February)
Open 10.00 am to 5.00 pm
with last admissions at 4.15 pm

Please telephone 020 7940 6300 for details of admission charges.

The new interactive 'Life at Sea' exhibition invites learners to test out their seamanship skills and listen to personal accounts of HMS *Belfast* veterans. Ideal for oral history, Citizenship and Literacy.

Above Girl Guides enjoying the facilities of sleepover on board HMS *Belfast*

Below left A young visitor trying on an original naval uniform during a school visit to HMS *Belfast*

Schools and youth groups can now 'Kip in a Ship' in 1950's restored messdecks experiencing life below decks and conditions at sea.

Refreshments

The Walrus Café in Zone 3 serves a variety of cooked meals, hot and cold drinks, snacks, sandwiches and confectionery.

Educational Services

From the crowded conditions of the hammock-slung messdecks to the re-creation of a great sea battle in the Operations Room, a visit to HMS *Belfast* provides a unique opportunity for children of all ages to learn about naval history and life at sea in the twentieth century. Our free learning programme of talks and hands-on activities is fun and flexible, designed to help deliver National Curriculum subjects.

Above One of the unique hospitality areas in HMS *Belfast*, awaiting the arrival of guests for a gala dinner

Above right HMS *Belfast*'s shop
Photograph: Glyn Williams

Opposite page, top
IWM Neg. No. HU 63914
Opposite page, bottom
IWM Neg. No. HU 69363

All of HMS *Belfast*'s educational services, including illustrated talks, films and hands-on activity sessions held in the Educational Facilities Suite are available free of charge to pre-booked school groups. A comprehensive Teachers Pack with information sheets and suggestions for work is available on request. For further details or to arrange a free preliminary visit, please contact the Education Officer on 020 7940 6323 / 020 7940 6336.

Please note that educational facilities are not available at weekends.

HMS *Belfast* has a packed lunch area capable of seating up to 25 children, with additional space on the upper deck for picnics in fine weather. The packed lunch area is also popular as a venue for birthday parties and parents can book a wide range of services, including special birthday teas, cakes and entertainment.
For further information, please contact the ship's Marketing Officer on 020 7940 6320.

Corporate Hospitality

HMS *Belfast* is an outstanding venue for both corporate and private entertainment.
The Admiral's Quarters, Wardroom and Anteroom, the Ship's Company Dining Hall, the Gunroom and the Quarterdeck can all be hired for receptions, lunches, dinners and conferences, and a full catering service is available. For further details and availability, please contact the Sales Office on
020 7403 6246
www.conference-online.co.uk
hms.belfast@sodexho.co.uk

Shopping and Mail Order

Available from HMS *Belfast*'s Gift Shop, and through a worldwide Mail Order service, are a wide range of publications including books, audio-visual material, postcards and educational resources, along with a selection of gifts and souvenirs for all the family.
For a free Catalogue of Publications, please write to:
Mail Order
Imperial War Museum Duxford
Cambridge CB2 4QR

Telephone 01223 499345 or
fax 01223 839688.

No admission ticket is required for entry to HMS *Belfast*'s Gift Shop, which is situated on the riverside embankment at the entrance to the ship.

Donations

It costs £1,000 a day just to preserve and maintain this great historic warship.
Donations are always welcome and should be addressed to:
Director, HMS *Belfast*, Morgan's Lane, Tooley Street, London SE1 2JH, or placed in the large black and white mine on the ship's Quarterdeck.